WISDOM TREE

Contents

1. **Curiosity** — 3
   Curiosity killed the cat.

2. **Team Spirit and Teamwork** — 9
   Alone, we can do so little; together, we can do so much.

3. **Gratitude** — 16
   When eating a fruit, think of the person who planted the tree.

   Managing Time — 23

4. **Self-Confidence** — 24
   If you think you are too small to make a difference, you haven't spent the night with a mosquito.

5. **Tolerance** — 31
   If you want to be respected, you will have to respect yourself.

6. **How to be a Leader** — 39
   To be a leader, you have to serve.

7. **Self-Control** — 46
   You know what you want, but do you know what you need?

   A Cleaner Greener Beautiful World — 54

   A Test of Your Values — 55

Curiosity

Do you ask questions? What is this? Why is it like this? Who got it here? Whom does it belong to? How do you use it?

You ask these questions because you are curious. You want to know about something. Sometimes, you want to know more about something. It is a good quality to be curious. Only when you are curious, do you discover and invent things.

Let us know more about curiosity, its benefits and its drawbacks from the following story.

The Story

The country of Kenya is famous for its wildlife sanctuaries, which are dotted with little villages around the boundaries.

A young boy called Richard Turere lived in one of these villages. As is the tradition in these villagers, boys between the ages 8 and 12 are responsible for the cattle belonging to their families. They take the cattle out for grazing and ensure that the cattle are all back by sunset. Naturally, the safety of these animals is also their responsibility.

Now, the villagers were facing a problem. Their village was close to a wildlife park. There were breaches in the boundary around the park. Lions came through these breaches in the dead of the night and attacked the village cattle. So, the village cattle were easy prey for the lions. Night after night, the lions would come into the village and hunt down the cattle.

Since Turere was responsible for his father's cattle, it was his duty to keep his cows safe. He was distraught to find the lions killing one cow after another. He started patrolling the grounds outside his house. To his delight, the lions did not dare to enter the grounds when he was around.

Thinking that the lions kept away sensing human presence, he put up a scarecrow to scare the lions away. Later, recalling his experience, Turere says, "The lions are very clever. They realize that the scarecrow is not a living thing. So they came into the cowshed and dragged away an animal to eat that night."

So now, Turere held a torch light in his hand and walked around his house. That night the lions did not come. They were scared.

Turere then realized that the light from the torch was scaring away the lions. So the next night, he tied his torch to a post and went to sleep. But the next morning, he saw that the lions had come and eaten away one more of his father's animals.

He wanted to find another way by which he could scare away the lions. Turere was not merely brave, but was also a curious child. When younger, he had removed all the parts of the radio at home to understand how it worked. And he succeeded in learning about it. It was another thing that his mother nearly beat-flogged him for dismantling the radio.

His curiosity made him understand and gain knowledge of how electronic things worked. That evening, he went about hanging some wires around his house. He attached some bulbs to these wires. Eventually, when night set in, he switched on his device. The bulbs around his house flashed on and off, one after the other.

That night the lions did not arrive. Neither did they bother him and his cattle ever again. To these lions, the flashing bulbs around Turere's house appeared as if people were walking about with torch lights. The lions mistook the flashing lights for people's movements.

Turere was applauded for his innovative idea. Many people across Kenya asked him for help to set up this simple system to save their cattle. He was also given a scholarship into one of the best schools of the country. His curiosity did indeed reward him well.

The other good thing that came about from his curiosity apart from his innovation is that the lions too were safe. Earlier, the traditional hunters in Kenya were forced to hunt down the lions that were killing their village cattle. Now, since the lions did not dare to come near the cattle, both the cattle and the lions were safe.

Have you understood the story? Now answer the following questions.

1. How did the village become a problem to the villagers?

2. What duty was Turere given by his family?

3. Why did Turere's idea of installing a scarecrow fail?

4. Why did Turere walk around his house in the night with a torch in hand?

5. Why had Turere dismantled his family radio?

6. Give examples to state that Turere was brave and curious.

More about the Value

It is good to be curious. When you are curious about people, you talk to them and become friends with them; or, you get to know more about them and stay away from them if you think they are not a source of good influence.

Likewise, when you are curious, you understand things better. For instance, if you are curious about electric wires and how they work, you ask an elder or pick up an encyclopaedia and read about it. And when you understand that it is dangerous to handle the wires, you take all precautions to be safe while handling them.

However, remember that you need to be extremely careful about the way in which you find answers to the things you are curious about. Take the same example of the electric wires. Remember, as a child you were asked to stay away from electric wires with wet hands. Did you ever ask why? Or, did you touch an electric wire with wet hands to see what happens? Obviously, you should ask why and understand why, rather than learn it through experience.

A VALUE FOR ME
Curiosity killed the cat.

Snippet

Isaac Newton was sitting under a tree. He was perhaps asleep, or he was perhaps thinking about something. And then, suddenly, an apple fell from the tree. We do not know whether it fell on him or near him. But he definitely felt the apple drop down from the tree.

This raised his curiosity. He wondered why an apple from a tree always fell straight down, but never to the side or why it never went up in the air.

The more he thought about it, the more curious he became. He observed that all objects always fell down to the earth but rarely flew away from the ground.

His curiosity made him think more and more, and he finally came up with the answer – Gravity.

He discovered that the earth's gravity pulled objects towards it like a magnet pulls pieces of metal towards it.

Newton's curiosity gave the world the concept of gravity. And because we know of gravity, we are able to build objects that challenge the concept of gravity and fly in the sky, and into outer space too.

Let Us Do

1. Which of the following statements are true? Mark your answer in the appropriate box.

   a. A curious person is active.   True / False

   b. A curious person is never bored.   True / False

   c. Curiosity is a dangerous thing.   True / False

   d. We should be cautious when we are looking for answers.   True / False

   e. Curiosity keeps our brain active because it makes us think.   True / False

2. Match the following words from the two columns. When you match them properly, you will be able to see how to keep your mind active and be a curious person.

Column A	Column B
Read different kinds of	boring without even trying it first.
Don't call something	search for their answers.
Think of learning	to make mistakes.
Ask questions and	books and magazines.
Never be afraid	as a fun activity.

3. Make a list of some things that you are curious about. Also mention how you plan to get your answers.

_____
_____
_____
_____
_____
_____
_____

Suggested Activities

Here are some activities that could develop your curiosity.

1. Go for a walk in a garden or a park. If possible, go trekking.
2. Visit new places with your family. New sights and new people will automatically pique your curiosity.
3. Solve puzzles. They will make you think and keep you active.
4. Get a hobby. Be it collecting stamps, shells or dried leaves, a hobby makes you curious.
5. Visit museums. They are the best places to see things from our past and from distant lands. They are places that offer a lot of information and kindle our interest in things.

Are you a curious person

1. Do you think of how things happen? Have you wondered about how the earth goes around the sun or why birds have wings but not hands?
2. Do you like to solve puzzles?
3. Do you ever go into the garden to see earthworms? Do you like to watch them move on their many legs?

* If the answer to all the above is 'yes', then you are a curious person. A curious person is never bored.

Tips to Parents and Teachers

Children are curious by nature. They will always have questions like 'how', 'what', 'when' and so on. As parents or teachers, we should never curb their curiosity. Instead of saying, "I don't know" or "please don't pester me with your questions", we could encourage their curiosity by saying, "Let us find out together, because even I do not know the answer to your question."

Do's and Don'ts

Be careful of how you find answers to your curiosity. You may be curious about what happens when a bee stings you. For this you could read it up on the Internet or in an encyclopaedia. But you need not find a bee and then deliberately get stung by it.

Team Spirit and Teamwork

Are you a part of a cricket team? Do you have houses in your school? Then you are a team member.

In a team, all the people play together to win the match or to win the house trophy. When every member works together, it is called teamwork.

When you are part of a team, you do not compete with other team members. You help each other. You do not fight with them. You do not create trouble for them so that they don't play or work well. You cheer them and support them. When you work by helping the other team members, you show team spirit.

Let us know more about team spirit and teamwork from the following story.

The Story

Long ago, in the jungles of India around the city of Kashi, there lived many wild animals. Though the jungles were dangerous because of the wild animals prowling in them, it did not stop the brave hunters from entering the jungles and spreading out their traps.

Once, one such hunter went into the jungle and spread a net. He wished to capture some exotic birds to be sold in the city.

When he finished securing his net at a desired spot, next to a lake, he made his way back to the village from where he came.

Early the next morning, a flock of beautiful birds flying by the jungle touched down by the lake. Having already eaten on their way, they wished to quench their thirst at the lake. Sadly, however, the minute the birds flew down, the net fell over them. Almost the entire flock of birds was caught in the net.

Some birds began to panic. "Oh, this is how we will all end!" cried some. "I am already suffocating. The net is very heavy on my wings," said another. In their fear, the birds started trying to fly here and there, trying to find a way out of the net.

The net was firm though. The net makers of Kashi were thorough professionals.

Amongst all the panic, one wise old bird in the flock spoke in his frail voice. "Listen to me, don't panic. It will not help us," he said.

However, none of the birds seemed to hear him. Even those who heard him, did not pay heed to him.

And then this old bird gathered all his might and shouted, "**LISTEN TO ME!**"

All the birds stopped whatever they were doing. They all turned in the old bird's direction.

And once again the old bird said, "Do not panic. It will do us no good."

Then one of the other birds in the flocks said, "What do you expect us to do if not panic. Should we wait silently for our death?"

The old bird replied, "No. We need not wait for our death at the hands of the hunter. We can escape if we work together. We can fly away with the net."

Some of the other birds in the flock started laughing at this. "What do you mean by flying away with the net?" said one. "Don't you know that the net is very heavy? We will never be able to take it with us," said another.

The wise old bird replied, "Don't worry. If we all take off at once, flapping our wings as one, we can easily carry the net with us. But remember that we have to work as a team. Everyone in the team has to use as much of their strength as they can. Only then is this task possible."

The birds, now hopeful that the old one's suggestion might give them back their freedom, flapped their wings when one of them gave them the go signal. And to their delight, the birds could rise themselves once again into the sky along with the heavy net.

They flew over the lake and reached the hole of a mouse. The mouse was an old friend of the birds. They told the mouse of how they came to be trapped in the net and how they flew away along with it because they flew together as a team. The mouse then called some of his family and together all the mice nibbled away at the strong nets.

Within no time, the nets were cut, the birds were free, the mice were thanked and a party to celebrate was organized.

Have you understood the story? Now answer the following questions.

1. Why did the birds panic?
   _____
   _____

2. Why did the birds make fun of the old bird when he asked them not to panic?
   _____
   _____

3. What was the suggestion that the old bird gave to win back the birds' freedom?
   _____
   _____

4. Why did the other birds initially think that the old bird's idea would not work?
   _____
   _____

5. What do you gather about teamwork from this story?
   _____
   _____

More about the Value

In your home, is only one person working all the time while the rest of the members lie around doing nothing? Or, is everyone helping each other in some way or the other? In the school, do you find a lot of people helping each other to run the school, or do you find only one person doing all the work in the school for it to run smoothly? Can you imagine your principal or your teacher coming in early to school to open the school gates, clean the building, buy all the chalks and papers needed in school as well as teach and then lock up the rooms in the evening? This is not the way a school functions. The people working in your school work as a team. Some do some jobs, others do some other work, and when they all do it together without disturbing the other, your school becomes a perfect school.

Another thing that is very important when working as a team is team spirit. Instead of competing with a team member, you have to make sure that you do your best for the team. You should never get lazy and stop doing something thinking that someone else in the team will do it. Only when all the team members do their work with honesty and dedication, will your team be the best.

'Swachch Bharat' is a team effort. When every citizen of our country stops littering the streets and uses a dustbin to throw waste, our country will become a clean country.

Together

        Everyone

                Achieves

                      More

A VALUE FOR ME

Alone, we can do so little; together, we can do so much.

Snippet

During the war in Vietnam, a US Captain, J. Charles Plumb, was lucky enough to eject himself from his fighter plane when it was struck down by the enemy. He was lucky to have safely landed and later return to his own country.

Many years later, when the captain was sitting at a restaurant sipping a cup of coffee, a man walked up to him and greeted him. Charles did not recognize the man because he had never met him. The stranger then said, "I was the one who had packed your parachute the day your plane was struck down." So saying, he walked away.

Charles was stunned. Over the years, since he had used his parachute, he had wondered many times what would have happened had his parachute not worked that day. Parachutes have to be packed very carefully and precisely. Else they would not open up. Many pilots had died not because their planes crashed but because their parachutes hadn't worked.

It was then that Charles realized how important teamwork and team spirit were.

As a pilot, he wouldn't be bothered with packing his parachutes, fuelling his plane or checking if the gadgets and engines in the planes were in condition. There were others to do these jobs. But without their complete involvement, dedication and sincerity, he wouldn't have been alive that day.

It was at that moment that he realized how a person's success is not merely his or her own but it is because of the work of many others.

Let Us Do

1. Fill in the blanks to complete the sentences. These sentences tell us about team spirit and teamwork. Choose your answers from the box.

   > Team mates   Friendly   One   All   Easier   Work

   a. When you _____ together, you can achieve even the most difficult goals.

   b. Working together makes your task _____.

   c. You should always help your _____.

   d. One for _____ and all for _____ explains team spirit.

   e. You should be _____ with all your team mates.

2. Which of the following require team spirit and teamwork? Circle your answers.

   a. A game of cricket
   b. A game of tennis (Singles)
   c. A game of chess
   d. Running a country
   e. Doing your homework
   f. Building a bridge
   g. Watering a plant

3. Read about how ants work as a team. Write a few lines about their team effort. Also list out what you can learn from them about team spirit.

   _____
   _____
   _____
   _____
   _____
   _____
   _____

14

4. Make a list of some activities in which you are involved that require teamwork. These activities could be those that you do in school, at your home or elsewhere.

_____
_____
_____
_____
_____
_____

5. Which of the following qualities are essential for teamwork? Circle your answers.

- Hard Work
- Participating
- Sharing
- Listening
- Respecting
- Being Selfish
- Secrecy
- Helping
- Jealousy
- Laziness

Do you have team spirit? Do you believe in teamwork?

1. Do you feel that you have to be better than the others in your team?
2. Do you like helping your team members?
3. If someone in your team scores a goal, do you feel jealous?
4. Do you talk and share with your team members?

*If the answers to the questions 1 and 3 are 'yes', then you are lacking on team spirit.

Tips to Parents and Teachers

Encourage children to play games that require children to be a part of a team. There is no better education than practical education. Encourage them to volunteer to help. Assign group projects both inside and outside school. For instance, you could encourage all the children in your building to help make their play ground neat. Being a part of a sports team or a group project can help your child develop the skills needed to work with others.

Do's and Don'ts

1. Always cheer for others in the team.
2. Do your best for the team.
3. Don't be lazy.
4. Don't think that you need not work because there are others in the team to do the work for you.
5. Respect all your team members.

Gratitude

When you thank someone for his or her help, you show gratitude. Gratitude is the quality of being thankful.

Gratitude also means returning kindness. When you realize that someone has been kind and helpful, you too should be helpful in return.

Read the following story to know more about the value of gratitude.

The Story

In ancient China, people used to store dried fish and rice to last them through the winter months when other food was scarce. Obviously, with harsh cold winds and snow everywhere, crops would be a rare sight and hunting is not always easy.

Like everyone else, Chang and his family also stored fish and rice for the approaching winter months. The fish were hung from the ceiling in the corner of their small home and the rice was stored in huge pots that were kept in pits dug up in the ground.

Now everyone loved the fish. Rice was bland and plain. Fish, on the other hand, was delicious and tempting. Moreover, since the fish were easily within reach, the members reached out for the fish and ate them often.

Soon, the stored fish

got over. There was only rice left. The year's winter seemed to be going on forever. People were wary about their survival. Many families had consumed their stock of rice as well.

In Chang's house, though the fish got over, they still had quite some rice left. At least Chang and his family would not starve.

Chang's grandmother, however, kept grumbling that there was no fish to eat. "I don't like to eat this rice. I want some fish."

Chang's father then told her gently to stop grumbling about the lack of fish. He said, "Mother, I understand that you are craving to eat fish. So are we. But we have to make do with the rice till spring arrives. Then, we will head out and bring you fresh fish."

The old lady kept on complaining. Finally, her son once again told her, "Mother, you need to understand that we are fortunate enough to have rice to eat. Many families in our village do not have that rice too. Be grateful for what you have."

Have you understood the story? Now answer the following questions.

1. Why did the ancient Chinese store fish and rice in their homes?
   _____
   _____

2. Why did everyone's fish get consumed faster than their rice?
   _____
   _____

3. What was Chang's grandmother complaining about?
   _____
   _____

4. What piece of advice did Chang's father give her?
   _____
   _____

More about the Value

We have learnt that gratitude is to be thankful for the help or kindness shown to us by others. Sometimes, we might not know who has helped us. One generation plants trees; the next enjoys the shade. So goes a Chinese proverb. Have you ever thought about whose orchard your juicy apple comes from? Have you ever thought of how much of hard work the farmer put in to grow the vegetables that you are eating?

> When eating a fruit, think of the person who planted the tree.

Gratitude also means that one should be thankful for what one has and not complain for what one does not have.

Finally, do you thank your teacher ever? Some children greet their teacher when the teacher enters the classroom and thank her when the teacher leaves the room. Have you wondered why you are thanking your teacher?

> If you can read this, thank a teacher.

There was once a woman who was miserable because she had lost one eye. She had only one eye to see the world with. Then, one day, she came across a person who had lost both his eyes. He could not see the world at all. It was then that she realized that though she had lost one eye, she was better off than the blind person. She could see with her remaining eye. She was grateful that she had at least one eye.

A VALUE FOR ME
Loose teeth are better than no teeth.

Let Us Do

1. Which of the following about gratitude are true? Tick or cross in the box accordingly.

    a. Saying 'Thank you' is a way of showing gratitude. ☐

    b. When you feel grateful, you feel sad. ☐

    c. Being kind and helpful to those you help you is also a way of showing your gratitude. ☐

    d. You should never let a person know that you are grateful for his or her help. ☐

    e. You are grateful only to people. You are not grateful to circumstances. ☐

    f. You feel nice when someone thanks you for your help. ☐

2. Be polite to everyone around you. Observe and be aware of what is happening around you. From now for a week, keep a record of when someone helps you or you feel grateful for something. Write it down in the following space. Also, mention whether you had said 'thank you.'

What I am grateful for	Whom I am grateful to	Did I say 'thank you'

When you have no one to thank but are thankful for your circumstances, you could thank God; or, write down what you are grateful for in a diary, at the end of the day.

3. **Fill in the blanks with appropriate words. They are all indicators on how you can be a grateful person. Choose your answers from the box.**

> Complain   Asked   Helped   Thank   Write

a. Help others without being _____.

b. _____ thank you notes to people who have given you gifts.

c. Remember to _____ all those who help you like your parents, teachers, the maid who works in your house, the boy who brings you your couriers and so on.

d. Make sure to help everyone, especially those who had _____ you.

e. Try not to _____ about what you don't have but be thankful for what you have.

4. **Name a few things in your life for which you are thankful. Count your blessings and be grateful.**

_____
_____
_____
_____
_____
_____
_____
_____
_____

5. **Which of the following persons do you think is grateful? Circle the correct options.**

   a. It is raining heavily. Salma has to walk through a slushy ground to get to her school. She is glad however that she has an umbrella so that she and her books don't get wet in the rain.

   Salma is grateful.   Salma is not grateful.

   b. Ridhima helped her younger brother to gather some leaves for his science project. Her brother thanked her.

   Ridhima's brother is grateful.   Ridhima's brother is not grateful.

   c. It is a very hot day. Pranav and Murali have to walk to the market to buy bread. Pranav is unhappy to walk in the hot sun. He goes on complaining all the way to the market. Murali, on the other hand, points out that there are lots of huge trees all along the path. He tells Pranav that it is not that hot when they walk in the shade of the trees.

   Pranav is grateful.   Murali is grateful.

Why should you be grateful?

When you have gratitude,

1. You will be a **happier** person
2. You will have **more friends**
3. You will be **liked** by more people
4. Chances are you will **not feel jealous**
5. You will be a **kinder** person
6. You will be a **healthier** person

Tips to Parents and Teachers

Merely saying 'thank you' does not mean that a person is grateful. Gratitude should come from within. It should be heartfelt. It should become a habit. Teach children to appreciate what they have, rather than crave for something that they do not have. Jealousy is what needs to be curbed. Children should be taught not to demand for things like toys or chocolates. Demanding and creating tantrums for such things should be discouraged. Rather, they should be taught to develop patience and self-control.

Do's and Don'ts

1. Always remember to thank those who have helped you.
2. Try to help everyone around you.
3. A kind act or a smile is also a way of showing someone that you are thankful for their help.
4. Never demand something by sulking or crying. When you get something like this and then say 'thank you', it doesn't show that you are grateful.

Managing Time

We all know that there are 24 hours in a day. Out of these 24 hours, we spend around 8 to 10 hours resting our body and mind. Rest is very important. You need to sleep on time and early. That way you will be able to wake up early too.

What you do with the rest of the day is up to you. You can read, play, eat, have fun, laze around, talk to friends, paint, and so on. But eventually, you need to follow a routine. You need to develop good and healthy habits. You need to do some things like bathe and eat every day. You need to do things like clean your room and study to grow wise.

Make a list of things you think need to be done every day in your life. Remember that you have only 24 hours in a day. So what you do and for how long you do these things will decide what kind of a person you will grow up to be.

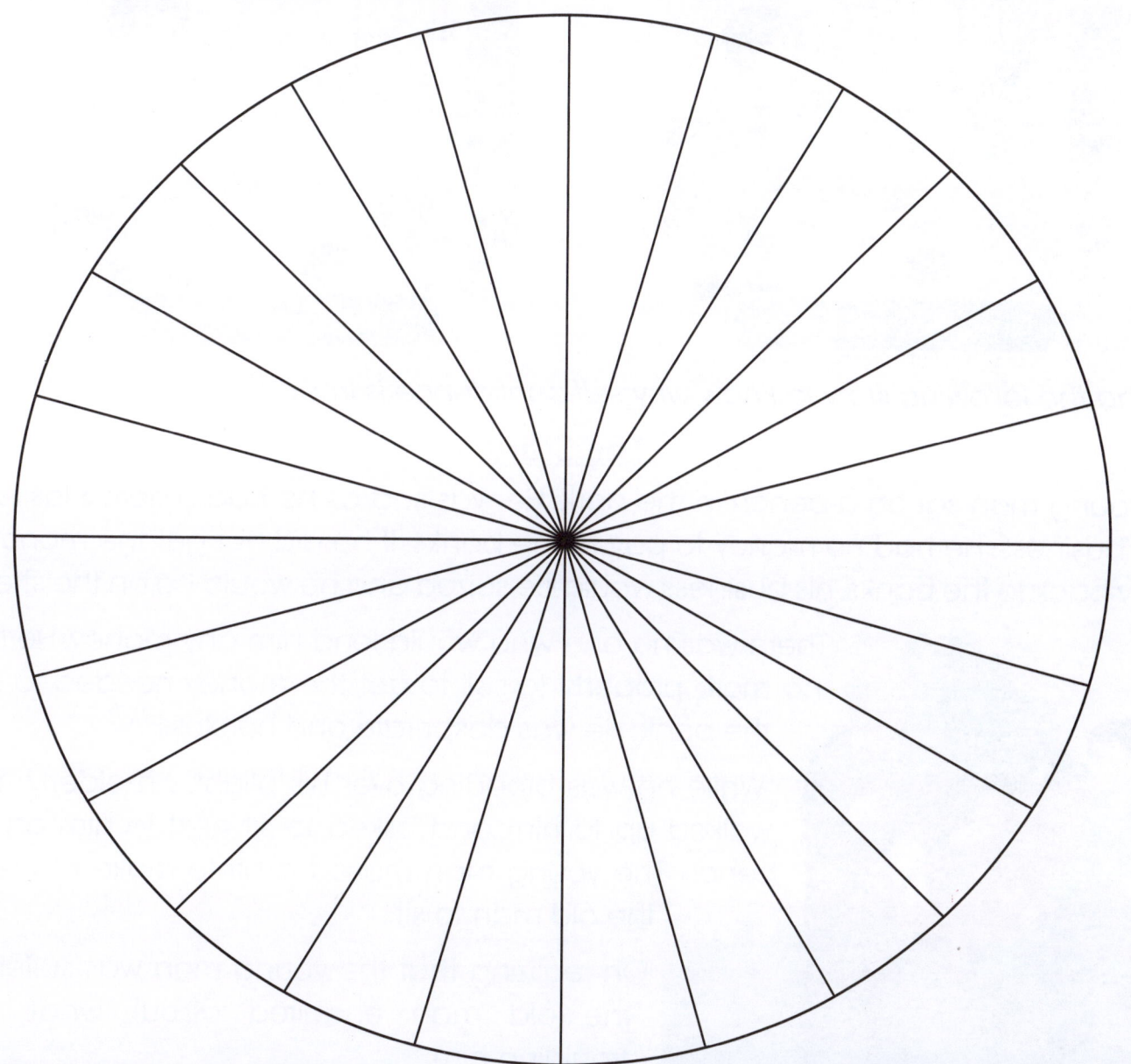

Self-Confidence

When you are sure that you can do a work, you are self-confident. When you know what you can do, you are self-confident. Self-confidence is also being able to trust yourself to do a work. In other words, you don't doubt yourself. Self-confidence is a very important value.

No self-confidence

Self-confident boy

Read the following story to know why self-confidence is important.

The Story

A young man sat on a bench in the park. He was sad as he had suffered losses in his business. He had no money to pay to the banks. If he did not get the money to pay back to the banks, his business would be seized and he would be on the streets.

There was no one who would lend him any money. He had no more property to sell to get the money needed to pay the bank. He was desperate and helpless.

While he was brooding over his plight, an elderly man walked up to him and asked to sit next to him on the bench. The young man moved a bit to make place for the old man to sit.

On realizing that the young man was suffering, the old man enquired about what was troubling him.

The young man then told the older person of his plight. After listening to the young man, the old man took out a cheque book from his coat pocket. He signed on it and handed it over to the young man. He said, "I hope this amount would be enough to help you clear your debts."

A nurse then walked up to the old man and said, "Oh there you are. It is time for us to return. Shall we go?" And she helped the old man to walk away, out of the park.

The young man was surprised to find a stranger handing him over a cheque for US$ 10,000. When he saw the name of the person on the cheque, he was shocked to see that none other than one of the richest persons in America, John D. Rockfeller, had given him the cheque.

With this gesture, the young man got back his confidence. He did not cash his cheque. He did not repay his debts with the cheque. Instead, he worked hard, came up with a solution to clear his debts on his own might and once again emerged successful in his business.

A few months later, the young man, now a happy and successful young man, walked into the park. He saw the same nurse who had helped Mr. Rockfeller out of the park. He went up to her and asked her how she was and how Mr. Rockfeller was. He said, "Can you tell me where to find Mr. Rockfeller? I need to return his cheque."

At this, the nurse said, "Are you referring to the person you saw with me in the park many months ago? He is not Mr. Rockfeller. He likes to call himself so. He is in fact a senile old man who does not remember who he is most of the time."

The young man was stunned. He realized that had he gone to the bank that day to cash the cheque, he would have known the truth immediately. He would then have lost his confidence once again. But thinking that a person like Mr. Rockfeller was behind him ready to offer him help, he had unknowingly gained an enormous amount of self-confidence and had accomplished what he had thought was impossible.

Have you understood the story? Now answer the following questions.

1. Why was the young man distressed?
   _____
   _____

2. Why did the old man give him a cheque?
   _____
   _____

3. Why do you think the young man did not cash the cheque and pay back his debts to the bank immediately?
   _____
   _____

4. What is the shocking truth about the old man that we get to know at the end of the story?
   _____
   _____

5. What does this story tell us about self-confidence?
   _____
   _____

More about the Value

Sometimes, we think we can do a work. However, we may not be able to do it. Can you think of any such incident? Can you share it with your friends in class?

Here is an example: Harry, along with his parents, went to the circus. When some acrobats performed somersaults, Harry's father said, "How wonderful!" Harry remarked, "Oh! I can somersault too. It is very easy." When Harry returned home, he tried to somersault. He could not.

When we think we can do a task though we may not have the strength or the knowledge to do it, we are not confident but we are overconfident. No doubt, Harry could very well learn to somersault, but till he learns to, he shouldn't talk of it. He should not boast that he could somersault. After all, the acrobats in the circus practiced for days and months to be able to somersault well.

It is important to know what you can do and what you cannot do. Once you know what you can do, you should not doubt yourself. You should tell yourself that you can do it and continue to do it well.

Remember, never be overconfident, and never doubt yourself too.

A VALUE FOR ME

If you think you are too small to make a difference, you haven't spent the night with a mosquito.

Snippet

Sir Winston Leonard Churchill was the Prime Minister of the United Kingdom twice, once from 1940 to 1945, and the second time from 1951 to 1956. Apart from being remembered as the Prime Minister of that country, he is also remembered as a great speaker.

But do you know that he was not always a very confident speaker? He was so afraid to reply to questions asked to him that he would stutter. Stuttering means to talk in such a way that the initial sounds of some words are repeated many times before the whole word is spoken.

How then do you think Churchill became such a great orator? It is said that to overcome his fear of not being able to respond well, he wrote speeches on many topics well before he was supposed to deliver them. He practiced speaking when alone and also read a lot to be able to answer any questions thrown at him.

Eventually, with all the practice and preparation, he became not only an eloquent speaker but also a very well learned man.

Let Us Do

1. Which of the following are true about a self-confident person?

    a. A self-confident person is capable of making decisions by himself or herself. [T] [F]

    b. A self-confident person is always doubting himself or herself. [T] [F]

    c. A self-confident person does not get tensed even in a difficult situation. [T] [F]

    d. Self-confident people are always scared and nervous. [T] [F]

    e. Self-confident people are not scared to try new things. [T] [F]

2. **Who among the following are self-confident? Tick your choice and cross out the rest.**

   a. It is Math Week and Anjana is excited to go to school. She has her pencils sharpened and ready in her bag. Monika, her classmate, is nervous. She is afraid that she might not be able to solve the puzzle and her classmates might then make fun of her.

   Anjana is self-confident. ☐

   Monika is self-confident. ☐

   b. Vandana, another of Anjana's classmates, is unable to answer a few questions in the puzzle. Even though there is half an hour left for the students to complete the puzzle, she turns in her paper. She doesn't want to attempt the difficult questions any more.

   Vandana is self-confident. ☐

   c. Radhika, who is in the same class as Anjana, is also unable to find answers to a few questions. She keeps trying to solve them though. She has half an hour more and she wants to see if she can solve the questions.

   Radhika is self-confident. ☐

3. Every person needs to have confidence in his or her own self. You can develop confidence in yourself by listing out some of your positive qualities. Make a list, be true to yourself and see how you feel about yourself.

Things I Like About Myself

4. What would you like to do in life? Do you have a goal? Do you think you can achieve the goal? How do you plan to achieve this? Write a few lines answering these questions. Later, read it out to your classmates. Reading out loud about yourself will not only develop your confidence, but will also motivate you to work towards achieving your goal.

   _____
   _____
   _____
   _____
   _____
   _____
   _____
   _____
   _____
   _____
   _____
   _____
   _____

5. Fill in the blanks to complete sentences that tell you more about how self-confident people behave.

   a. Self-confident people don't _____ to ask for help.

   b. Self-confident people don't make _____ of others.

   c. Self-confident people _____ up their mistakes.

   d. Self-confident people say _____ to what they think is wrong. They are not afraid.

   e. Self-confident people are not _____ of losing. Even when they lose, they try to learn out of their mistakes.

Are You a Self-Confident Person?

Which of these statements are true about yourself?

1. I like myself a lot.
2. At times, I feel I am not good at all. I hate myself then. I wish I could be someone else.
3. I know what I am good at and what I cannot do.
4. I am proud of myself.
5. I am not proud of myself at all.

* If you feel that statements 1, 3 and 4 are true, then you are a self-confident person.

Tips to Parents and Teachers

Each child has his or her own pace of development. Some are slow while others are fast. Some pick up a concept on one reading, while others take more than one reading to understand a concept. Some are good at sports while others are good at art. Identify the uniqueness in each child and encourage them. Comparing them with others will only deflate their self-confidence.

Do's and Don'ts

1. Never doubt yourself, but be humble.
2. Never belittle others.
3. Help others if you can while doing your own work.
4. Be cheerful always.

Tolerance

We have learnt earlier that we are all different. We speak different languages and practice different religions; we dress differently and we also have different skin colours. Tolerance is the quality to respect the difference in the other person. To be able to love your own religion or language while not hating someone else's religion or language is called tolerance.

Tolerance is also the ability to remain calm and not get angry with someone for behaving differently.

Read the following story to know more about tolerance.

The Story

The people of Maharashtra narrate a story that they believe to have really taken place. They say that once their famous king, Chhatrapati Shivaji, while riding his horse through a forest, was hit on the forehead by a large stone.

Blood started trickling down his face. Though he was hurt, he was a trained warrior and he could tolerate the pain. However, he became furious at the thought that someone had the courage to throw a stone at him.

He had the few soldiers travelling with him search around to see who the culprit was. Soon, one of the soldiers brought forward an old woman. When Shivaji saw that it was a frail, old, innocent-looking woman, he doubted that she would have had the courage to throw the stone at him. He asked her, "Old lady, have you seen the person who threw the stone at me?"

The old lady replied, "O King, I had thrown the stone at you. It was a mistake. Please forgive me. I did not meant to hurt you. In fact, the stone was not even meant to be thrown anywhere near you. I was merely throwing the stones at the huge mango tree so that some mangoes might fall down. I want to take the delicious mangoes back to the village for my family.

"Unfortunately, just when I had aimed the stone at the tree, you happened to pass from underneath that very tree. Please forgive me."

When Shivaji heard the woman out, he calmed down. His early fury had all evaporated. He then realized that if a mighty mango tree, despite being hit by large stones year after year, continued to give the sweet fruit, he too should be benevolent and forgiving. He too should learn to be tolerant just as the tree is and continue to do his work though people might fling accusations at him or try to hinder his work.

He let the woman go back to her family. But before he let her go, he asked his soldiers to pluck a basket full of ripe mangoes for the woman to take them back to her family.

Have you understood the story? Now answer the following questions.

1. How was Shivaji hurt?
   _____
   _____

2. Why was Shivaji furious on being hurt?
   _____
   _____

3. Why did Shivaji not suspect the old woman?
   _____
   _____

4. Why did Shivaji think that the mango tree was tolerant?
   _____
   _____

5. If Shivaji perceived the tree to be tolerant, what other value(s) do you think he could have learnt from the old woman?
   _____
   _____

More about the Value

By now, you must have understood that tolerance is the ability to respect others and their differences. It is the ability to understand that they can behave differently and we should not get agitated by it.

To be tolerant, you should first understand that people are different. You should understand how they are different. You should also understand that it is okay to be different.

When you respect others despite them being different from you, or behaving differently from what you expect, they too will begin to respect you for your difference.

A VALUE FOR ME

If you want to be respected, you will have to respect yourself.

Snippet

Jesse Owens was the son of farm workers and the grandson of slaves in the United States of America. Fortunate enough not to have been born in the era of slavery in the USA, Jesse went to school and college, and got himself educated.

While in college, he managed to break one field and track events world record, and equaled three others. He was selected to represent his country in the 1936 Olympic Games to be held in Germany.

It was a strange time then. The world was in between two World Wars. People were still discriminating against the blacks in the US. In Germany, Adolf Hitler was trying to prove that the Aryan race was the most superior race in the world. There wasn't much tolerance in the air.

In the 1936 Olympic Games, Jesse managed to win four gold medals, a phenomenal feat. However, sadly, in a world full of prejudices and discrimination, it is said that Adolf Hitler was furious that a black had out run the whites. It is said that Hitler had walked out of the stadium in anger.

Later, when Jesse returned to his home country, he remarked, "When I came back to my native country, after all the stories about Hitler, I couldn't ride in the front of the bus. I had to go to the back door. I couldn't live where I wanted. I wasn't invited to shake hands with Hitler, but I wasn't invited to the White House to shake hands with the president, either."

Let Us Do

1. **Choose the correct option.**

   a. Your friend is a Muslim. You are a Sikh. He calls you home on Eid for a party. You don't pray to Allah, so should you go or not go for the party?

      i. You should go ☐

      ii. You should not go ☐

   b. Mira is a vegetarian. Koel eats non-vegetarian food. They both argue about their food choices.

      Mira: I cannot understand how you can kill animals to eat food. Please do not sit next to me while eating your non-vegetarian food.

Koel: You will not get enough proteins from your vegetarian food. I cannot understand how you can manage to eat only leaves and vegetables.

Who is being intolerant?

a. Mira ☐   b. Koel ☐   c. Both Mira and Koel ☐

2. **Complete the following sentences to solve the crossword below. All these sentences teach you how to be a tolerant person.**

   a. You should think of the _____ in others and this will help you to develop tolerance.

   b. _____ in yourself first.

   c. _____ from others.

   d. Accept that people are _____.

   e. Don't make _____ of other cultures.

   f. _____ others the way you want to be treated.

b. B _ _ _ _ _ _ c. L _ _ E _ _ E
a. _ O O _
d. _ _ _ _ e. F _ F F E _ E _ _ E N f. T

3. Make a list of five of your close friends. Then write one thing that you share in common with each of your friends and one thing that you dislike about your friend or which is different about your friend. Then ponder if this difference or dislike has ever stopped you from being a friend to that person.

My friend's name	What I have in common with my friend	What I dislike about my friend / How my friend is different from me

4. Which of the following people are being tolerant? Tick the correct boxes and cross out the others.

a.

I don't like watching TV with you. You see boring programmes all the time.

The grandchild is tolerant.   The grandchild is intolerant.

b.

Sam, I love reading the 'Harry Potter' Series.

Steve, I hate the books. I don't believe in magic. But since you like them, I will buy you one for your birthday.

Sam is tolerant.   Sam is intolerant.

Are you a tolerant person?

1. Do you get irritated when people don't do things your way?

2. Do you insist that people agree with you? Do you go on arguing till the other person agrees with you?

3. Do you treat others the way you want to be treated?

4. Do you judge people? Do you call them good or bad without thinking why they have to behave the way they do?

5. Do you ever agree to others' suggestions even though you don't like them?

*If your answers to the questions 1, 2 and 4 are 'yes' then you need to work on becoming more tolerant. You have to understand that people are different. They have different opinions. They work differently from us. Therefore, it is not always necessary that they have to do things your way or agree with you at all times.

Tips to Parents and Teachers

Point out to children that everyone is special in his or her own way. People should not be discriminated based on skin colour, nationality or culture.

Also, children should be taught to respect the other person despite their differences. Branding a child as good or bad, naughty or clever, slow or fast does not help in instilling tolerance. Instead, teach them to appreciate the goodness in the other person.

Do's and Don'ts

1. Never force your thoughts onto someone. You can advice and suggest but not force them to do things your way.

2. Most of the time, there is no good or bad about someone else's religion, language, food or culture. They may just be doing it differently.

3. Being tolerant does not mean you have to listen to the other person all the time. You may have your views and the other person may have his views. You may believe in Jesus and the other person may believe in Krishna. As long as you force the other person to stop praying to Krishna or Jesus, you are a tolerant person. At the same time, you don't have to stop believing in your god to show that you are tolerant.

How to Be a Leader

Leading a group of people is leadership. When you wish to be a leader, you need some qualities. People should respect you. They should not hate you. They should listen to you. You should be able to make the right decisions for your team. These and many more qualities make you a good leader.

Leadership is an important quality that you need to learn because it comes in handy to you when you are leading your team.

The Story

There is a bridge in New York, USA that connects the Manhattan Island to the area called Brooklyn. Built nearly 120 years ago, this bridge is considered to be an engineering marvel and miracle. In 1863, an engineer named John Roebling came up with an idea to build this bridge. Other engineering experts however thought that this bridge was not feasible. They declared that it was not possible to build this bridge.

However, so convinced was Roebling that this bridge could be built that he asked his son Washington to help him build the bridge. The two of them spent years in designing and planning the bridge. Their understanding and planning of the bridge had to be thorough before they could take up this difficult task. Eventually, when all their planning was complete, they hired construction crew and began to build the bridge.

A few months passed. Barring a few difficulties, the project was going on smoothly. Sadly, Roebling was involved in an accident on the site of the bridge and he died. His son, the only other engineer who understood the project thoroughly, was also involved in this accident. And he lost his ability to talk and walk. He could in fact move only one finger on his own.

The Roeblings were the only two engineers who knew how to build the bridge. With one of them dead and the other in no position to monitor or guide the construction, people thought that the bridge would no longer be built.

But so determined was Washington to see to the completion of the bridge, that he developed a code of communication. He used the one finger that he was able to move to tap onto his wife's arm. His wife then decoded the message that he was tapping onto her arm and explain it to the other engineers present to help build the bridge.

How long do you thing Washington tapped messages onto his wife's arm? For thirteen years! For thirteen years, Washington relentlessly gave instructions with one finger and saw to it that the bridge was completed.

Washington was determined, resourceful and innovative. Such was his greatness and leadership.

Have you understood the story? Now answer the following questions.

1. What project did Roenbling decide to undertake?
   _____
   _____

2. Why did he have to rope in his son to help him build the bridge?
   _____
   _____

3. How were the father and son affected by the tragic accident on site?
   _____
   _____

4. What was the extent of physical impairment that Washington suffered?
   _____
   _____

5. What was the innovative way in which Washington communicated with his wife? For how long did he continue to give instructions for the construction of the bridge through this method of communication?
   _____
   _____

More about the Value

What does a good leader do? He or she:
- Decides the best path for the entire team
- Helps the team members to achieve what they are meant to do
- Gives advice to the team members
- Behaves in such a way that all team members are inspired by him or her
- Supports his or her team member

Being a leader does not mean that you get others to do the work for you. On the contrary, you are expected to work for others at all times.

> "I never thought in terms of being a leader. I thought very simply in terms of helping people." – John Hume

Being a leader does not mean that you are better than the others in the team. Consider the Indian cricket team. The captain is not always the best batsman, the best bowler or the best wicket-keeper. The captain is one who can guide the rest of the team, motivate the players, encourage them and make decisions for the team. A good captain remembers to consult his or her teammates and makes the decisions keeping in mind the entire team's welfare.

Snippet

Many a song has been sung in praise of the valiant warrior leader, Rani of Jhansi. She was born in the city of Kashi, now Benaras, in the year 1828. She was called Manikarnika in her younger days. Her mother died when Manikarnika was merely 4 years old. Her father raised her. Along with getting her educated, he also taught her to ride horses and to fight with various weapons. When she grew up, her father got her married to Gangadhar Rao, the king of Jhansi.

She was called the Rani Lakshmi Bai after her marriage. The king and the queen had a son, but the baby died when he was four months old. The couple then adopted a boy. According to Hindu law, the adopted son was to become the king in future. But when Gangadhar Rao died, the British, who were then occupying India, decided that the adopted boy will not become the king. They ordered that the state of Jhansi was to be handed over to the British.

But the queen refused to do so. She raised an army of volunteers. She personally trained women who wanted to safeguard their kingdom and stop it from falling into the hands of the British.

Rani Lakshmi Bai led her army personally on the battlefield. She not only tried to ward off the British but also kept the neighbouring kingdoms of Orjha and Datia from invading.

Though she fought valiantly, she was eventually killed in battle and her kingdom went over the British.

Despite the defeat, she is praised as one of the bravest and most dedicated leaders of our country.

Let Us Do

1. Consider you are a leader. Which of the following lines are you most likely to say? Tick the correct ones and cross out the wrong ones.

    a. Yes, we can do it.

    b. I don't know what to do. I will give up.

    c. This is difficult. Let us not even try it.

d. This is difficult. Nevertheless, let us try to do it. By working hard, we may be able to do it. ☐

e. I will do my best to help all the team members. ☐

f. I am the leader. So I don't have to do any work. The rest of the team will work for me. ☐

g. We have made a mistake. No problem. Let us try again and do it correctly this time. ☐

2. **What are you supposed to do as a leader? Fill in the blanks with the correct words from the box.**

| Properly | Angle | Doubt | Think | Inspire |

a. A leader should _____ all the team members to do their best.

b. A leader should be able to think every _____ possible.

c. A leader should always _____ that the target is possible.

d. A leader should not be in _____. He or she should be able to decide what they and their team members should do.

e. A leader should be able to talk and convey his or her ideas to everyone _____.

3. **Stick pictures of your favourite leaders. Mention, along with their names, the team or country that they lead. Your leaders could be political leaders, sports captains, your school captains and so on. Also mention one quality in them that you like the most.**

4. **If you were to become the Prime Minister of the country, you will have the power to change the country or lead it according to your ideas. What will you do or not do to improve the country? Write down your thoughts.**

As the Prime Minister of this country, I will _____
_____
_____
_____
_____

Further, I will not _____
_____
_____

Can you be a good leader?

- Volunteer to help others or take a leadership position in your class.
- Listen more and be more helpful at home and with your siblings.
- Join a team or an organization like the Cub Scouts, Boy Scouts or Girl Scouts. They are all about building leadership skills.
- Think about what you can do to improve your leadership skills. Consider using this worksheet to set some goals for yourself.

Remember, if the team performs well, it is because of the hard work of the entire team, but if something goes wrong, the leader should be ready to take the blame.

Tips to Parents and Teachers

The key skills of having vision, developing determination and discovering the passion and strength to carry out any task come with independence. Rather than guiding the child through every activity, parents and teachers should step back a little and allow children to explore and work independently. No doubt, a watchful eye can be on them, but it needs to be done discretely. Allowing children to make their own mistakes will also give them a chance to learn from those mistakes and improve themselves.

Do's and Don'ts

1. Never boss around.
2. Listen to your team members but decide what is best for them.
3. Work along with the team.
4. You don't have to shout at people to get them to listen to you.

Self-Control

Did you ever want an ice cream but stopped yourself from eating it because you had a cold? Did you do it by yourself or did you do it because you were told by someone?

When you tell yourself the right thing to do before someone else does, you have self-control.

Read the following story to know why self-control is important.

The Story

Socrates was from ancient Greece. He was and is still well known for his wisdom.

One day, a man walked up to Socrates and said, "I have heard something about your friend. Wouldn't you want to know?"

Though he asked Socrates a question, he had every intention of gossiping about Socrates' friend to him.

Before the man could begin what gossip he wished to share, Socrates raised his hand and said, "My dear man, before you tell me what you wish to, I would like you to pass a test."

The man was taken aback. 'Why must I pass a test to speak something?' he thought. However, since Socrates was well regarded by all in the city, he decided to listen to him. "All right, I will take this test. But pray tell me, what this test is about."

Socrates replied, "I call this the triple filter test. You need to answer three questions before you can tell me anything about my friend."

The man agreed to take the test.

Socrates' first question to the man was:

"Are you absolutely sure that what you are about to tell me is indeed true?"

The man hesitated a minute before saying, "I cannot say. Actually, I heard someone say…"

Socrates cut the man mid-sentence and said, "Hmm, so you don't know if it is the truth. Well here is my second question. Is what you are going to tell me about my friend something good?"

Once again, the man hesitated and said, "No. In fact, it is quite the opposite."

Socrates then replied, "Those two were the tests of truth and goodness. My final test is that of usefulness. Is what you are about to tell me going to be useful to me?"

The man, as you can realize by now, said, "No, …"

Immediately, Socrates declared that the man had failed the triple filter test. Since the man had failed the test, Socrates refused to listen to what the man had to tell him.

When something is not true, not good or not useful, there is no need to encourage or indulge in it. If we are all able to apply the triple filter test to everything in our life, and then stick by the results, we would not only be showing great self-control, but we will also be leading a fuller and more positive life.

Have you understood the story? Now answer the following questions.

1. Why did Socrates stop the man from talking about Socrates' friend?

2. What is Socrates' first test called? What was the question?

3. What is Socrates' second test called? What was the question?

4. What is the third test called? What was the question?

5. How would applying the triple filter test be a mark of self-control?

More about the Value

Self-control is not only stopping yourself from eating what you want to, but also controlling your emotions. When you receive presents on your birthday, you are naturally very curious to see what is inside the gift wrapping. Do you tear them open immediately or wait till the party is over and your guests have left? If you can wait till your guests have left, you have self-control.

Self-control is also the ability to remain calm even when you feel anger. To be able to do the right thing even though it is difficult is also having self-control.

A VALUE FOR ME
You know what you want, but do you know what you need?

Snippet

Karna, the king of Anga, and a friend of Duryodhana, was a person with great self-control. Once, while he was getting educated at the gurukul, his teacher wanted to rest. Since there was no pillow around, Karna offered his thigh as the pillow.

The guru fell asleep on Karna's lap. Sometime later, while the teacher was still asleep, a scorpion crawled near Karna. Karna saw the scorpion, but did not flinch. He did not move. He did not want to disturb his guru.

The scorpion bit into Karna's thigh. Even then Karna did not move. Though his thigh was now burning from the scorpion's bite, he did not move an inch because he did not want to disturb his teacher. Such was his self-control.

Let Us Do

1. Here is a list of some activities that you might do every day. Tick all those in which you need to show self-control.

    a. Reaching school on time ☐

    b. Eating a healthy breakfast ☐

c. Sneaking a snack out of the box while the teacher is still teaching because you are very hungry ☐

d. Following traffic rules ☐

e. Waiting for the break to use the restroom ☐

f. Walking in neat lines to the assembly ☐

g. Over eating because you love the taste of the item ☐

h. Waking up early and sleeping on time ☐

i. Sitting straight while eating your food ☐

j. Sleeping on the bed while reading your comics even though you should not read while sleeping ☐

k. Reducing the volume of the TV because your grandparents are sleeping ☐

2. To be able to sing with others in a choir or to play an instrument in a band, you need self-control. You have to know when to sing a line, how long to sing a line and in what key to sing the song. If you do not follow the rules and sing the song in whichever way you want to, it is no longer a pleasant choir. Therefore, participate in school choirs, school bands and sports teams to learn self-control.

3. Are you familiar with fairy tales? Which of the following fairy tale characters showed self-control? Tick your answers and cross out the others.

   a. Goldilocks when she ventured into the woods all by herself and then ate from the bowl of porridge. ☐

b. Snow White when she bit the apple the witch gave her.

c. Cinderella when she continued to keep a clean home even though her stepmother and -sisters were cruel to her.

d. Pinocchio when he told lies.

e. Little Red Riding Hood when she spoke to the wolf even though her mother told her not to speak to strangers. ☐

4. Create a timetable for your daily chores. Make sure that you follow the timetable every day. Remember, it takes great self-control to do your work on time or as planned.

For every task that you perform on time, put a tick mark against it. You could do your review at the end of the day. Follow this for at least a week.

The Task	Time Slot	Am I Successful?				
		Mon	Tue	Wed	Thu	Fri
Waking up in the morning						
Breakfast						
Leaving for school						
Homework time						
Play time						
Dinner						
Sleeping at night						

5. Most of your behaviour shows whether you have self-control or not. Colour those boxes that show that you have self-control.

- Responding when someone calls out your name
- Sleeping on time and waking up on time
- Getting angry and showing it too
- Eating at regulated times only
- Eating whenever you feel like it
- Sitting in a correct posture
- Thanking people when they help you
- Interrupting a conversation with the phrase 'excuse me'
- Standing in a queue and waiting for your turn
- Shouting at someone who has hurt you

Do you have self-control?

1. Do you get angry easily? When you get angry, do you

    a. shout at others or break things?

    b. try to be calm and get your temper down?

2. If you were to choose between eating a pizza and idli, what would you do? Remember, you have been told that a pizza is junk food and idli is one of the healthiest foods in the world.

   a. Choose pizza for this one time because it is tastier than idli. ☐

   b. Choose idli because it is healthy and you want to eat healthy food. ☐

3. It is very hot. You want to go swimming but you cannot because your parents asked you not to go while your sister is still suffering from cold. What do you do?

   a. You do not go to the pool. You sit at home and give your sister company. ☐

   b. You go to the pool on the sly without letting your sister know where you are going. ☐

Read out your answers in class and ask your friends if your choice of answers shows that you have self-control.

Tips to Parents and Teachers

Acknowledge and compliment a child's effort in showing self-control. Whenever you notice that the child has refrained from doing something despite being tempted, tell them that you have noticed their effort and are proud of their action or choice.

Also, when the child needs to stay away from things, it would help them if you too stay away from it, along with the child. For instance, if the child is trying to show self-control in not watching a favourite TV show because he or she has to finish his school work, you as a parent should also stop yourself from watching the show. This will help the child to better focus on the task at hand and not get tempted by it.

Do's and Don'ts

1. Understand what is good and what is bad for you. Always think before you act.
2. When you know that something is not to be done, try your best not to do it.
3. Don't ever do something without thinking. You may repent later.

A Cleaner, Greener and Beautiful World

Most of us live in cities, towns or villages. We live in houses made of brick. We have manmade roads to drive on, pavements to walk on, fences around our gardens, and other houses or factories to look at.

But there are many places around the world which are not yet occupied by man. There are places where man has not yet built anything. These are places which are still in their natural state. Many of them are stunning, beautiful and give us peace and joy when we see them.

Collect some pictures of such places and stick them here. Treasure these places and try to leave them as they are without polluting them.

A Test of Your Values

Solve the crossword puzzle to check your values.

Here are the clues:

Across:

1. An eye for an eye will make the world _____.
2. It pays to be _____.
5. _____ is the best policy.
6. _____ is worship.
7. _____ people of all ages and religions. Be tolerant.
12. _____ is impossible.

Down:

2. To be a leader you have to _____.
3. A _____ in need is a friend indeed.
4. When eating a fruit, _____ of the person who planted the tree.
7. The more you _____, the more you acquire.
8. To love one's country is called _____.
9. _____ begins with a smile.
10. Curiosity killed the _____.
11. _____ is strength.
13. _____ others whenever you can.
14. United we stand, _____ we fall.

Collect some pictures of such places and stick them here. Treasure these places and try to leave them as they are without polluting them.

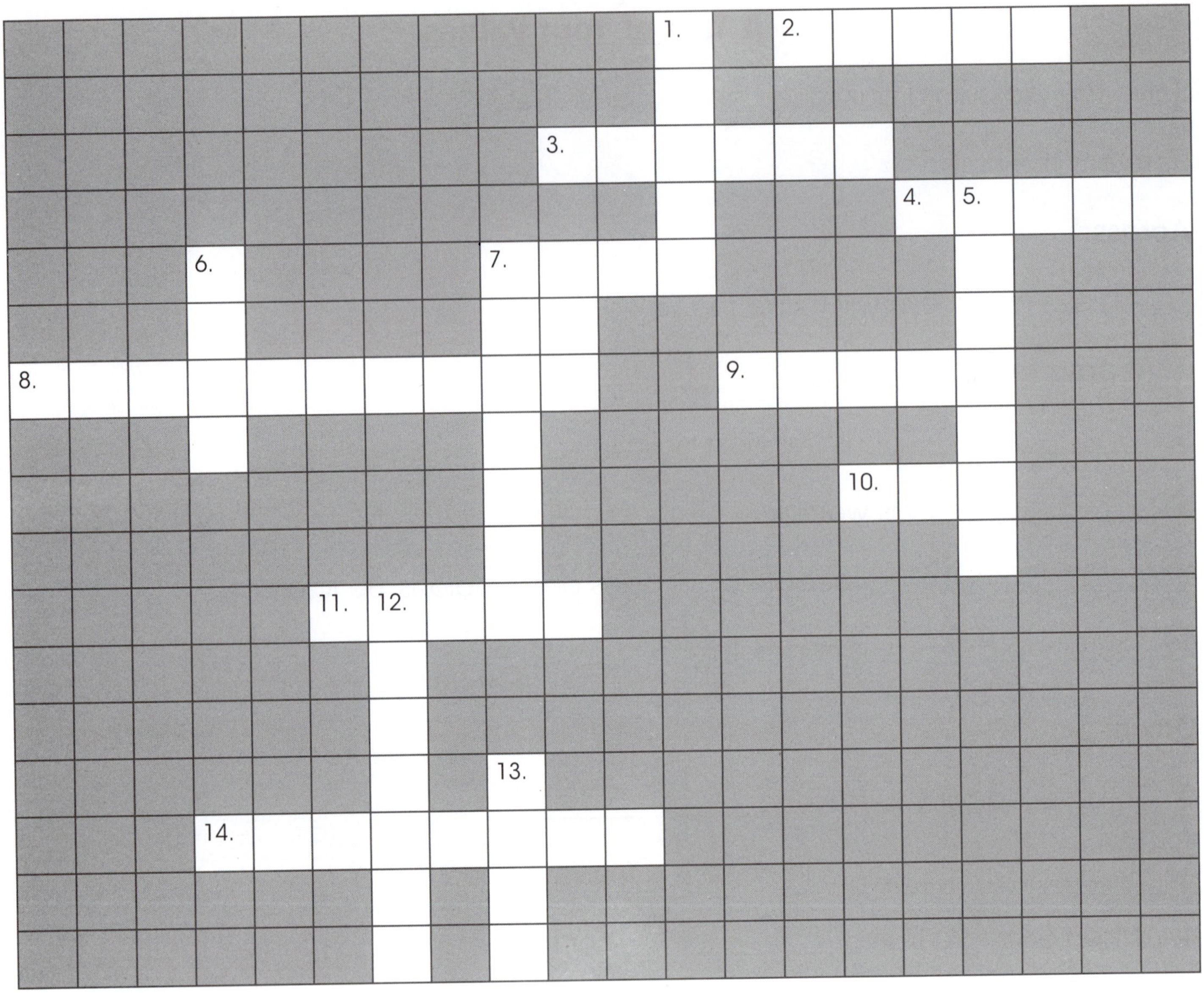
1.
2.
3.
4.
5.
6.
7.
8.
9.
10.
11.
12.
13.
14.